"I pray that you will have greater understanding in your heart. Then you will know the hope that God has chosen to give us. I pray that you will know that the blessings God has promised his holy people are rich and glorious."

- Ephesians 1:18 (ICB)

*To my husband Peter and our four children,
Calem, Abram, Hayden & Hope.
May you always have a strong prayer life and a
close relationship with God.
-T. Z.*

Copyright© 2021 Tatiana Zurowski

All rights reserved. No part of this publication may be reproduced, stored in a retrieval system, or transmitted in any form or by any means, electronic, mechanical, photocopying, recording or otherwise, without written permission of the publisher. Published by

Harvested Works Group LLC
8584 Washington St., #2015
Chagrin Falls, OH 44023-5369

Scripture quotations marked (NIV) are taken from the Holy Bible, New International Version®, NIV®. Copyright © 1973, 1978, 1984, 2011 by Biblica, Inc.™ Used by permission of Zondervan. All rights reserved worldwide. www.zondervan.comThe "NIV" and "New International Version" are trademarks registered in the United States Patent and Trademark Office by Biblica, Inc.™ Scripture taken from the International Children's Bible®. Copyright © 1986, 1988, 1999 by Thomas Nelson. Used by permission. All rights reserved. Scripture quotations marked NLV are taken from the New Life Version, copyright © 1969 and 2003. Used by permission of Barbour Publishing, Inc., Uhrichsville, Ohio 44683. All rights reserved. Scripture quotations marked NLT are taken from the Holy Bible, New Living Translation, copyright © 1996, 2004, 2015 by Tyndale House Foundation. Used by permission of Tyndale House Publishers, Inc., Carol Stream, Illinois 60188. All rights reserved.

ISBN Number: 978-1-7375908-0-4 (Paperback)
ISBN Number: 978-1-7375908-1-1 (Hardback)
Library of Congress Control Number: 2021915230

HOW TO PRAY
TRAIN UP ARROWS

Written by Tatiana Zurowski
Illustrated by HH-Pax

Come along children, it's time to pray,
even if you don't know what to say.
You can follow the steps that are laid out here,
and learn to pray with no need to fear.

"In the same way, the Holy Spirit helps us where we are weak. We do not know how to pray or what we should pray for, but the Holy Spirit prays to God for us with sounds that cannot be put into words."

– Romans 8:26 (NLV)

You can start off with praises to God,
at first, it may seem a little odd.
You call Him magnificent names,
some of which might mean the same.
Almighty Father, King of kings,
Healer, Provider, and other kind things.

"I will praise you as long as I live, and in your name I will lift up my hands."
- Psalm 63:4 (NIV)

Next, you can confess your sins,
especially ones you have bottled in.
Anything you've thought, said, or done,
that may cause pain in the long run.
Ask the Lord for His forgiveness,
then try your best to be a witness.

"But if we confess our sins, he will forgive our sins. We can trust God. He does what is right. He will make us clean from all the wrongs we have done."

- 1 John 1:9 (ICB)

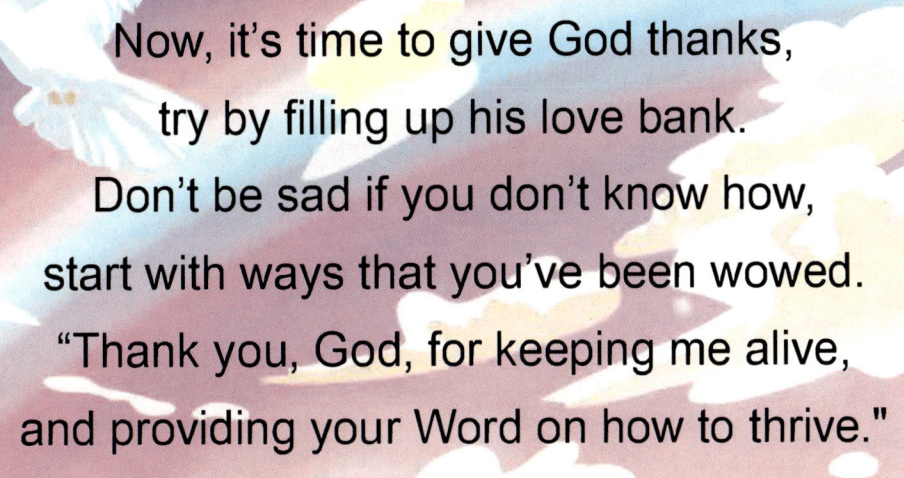

Now, it's time to give God thanks,
try by filling up his love bank.
Don't be sad if you don't know how,
start with ways that you've been wowed.
"Thank you, God, for keeping me alive,
and providing your Word on how to thrive."

"I will give thanks to you, Lord, with all my heart; I will tell of all your wonderful deeds."
- Psalm 9:1 (NIV)

Praying for others is next on the list,
even if they've hurt you, you must persist.
Those are the ones who need prayer now,
never give up and let them down.

You can pray for family, friends, and even strangers,
or perhaps world leaders to protect them from dangers.
Pray they have love, peace, and joy,
and maybe even a brand-new toy.

MEXICO | SAUDI ARABIA | THE REPUBLIC OF KOREA | THE UNITED KINGDOM | THE EUROPEAN UNION

"First, I tell you to pray for all people. Ask God for the things people need, and be thankful to him. You should pray for kings and for all who have authority. Pray for the leaders so that we can have quiet and peaceful lives—lives full of worship and respect for God."

- 1 Timothy 2:1-2 (ICB)

"But the Holy Spirit produces this kind of fruit in our lives: love, joy, peace, patience, kindness, goodness, faithfulness, gentleness, and self-control. There is no law against these things!"
- Galatians 5:22-23 (NLT)

"We are sure that if we ask anything that He wants us to have, He will hear us. If we are sure He hears us when we ask, we can be sure He will give us what we ask for."
- 1 John 5:14-15 (NLV)

God always has the final word,
just stand on faith and feel secured.

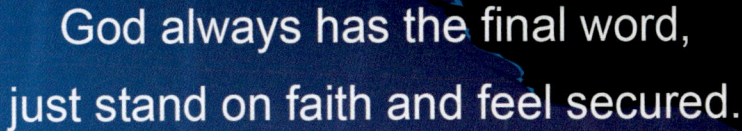

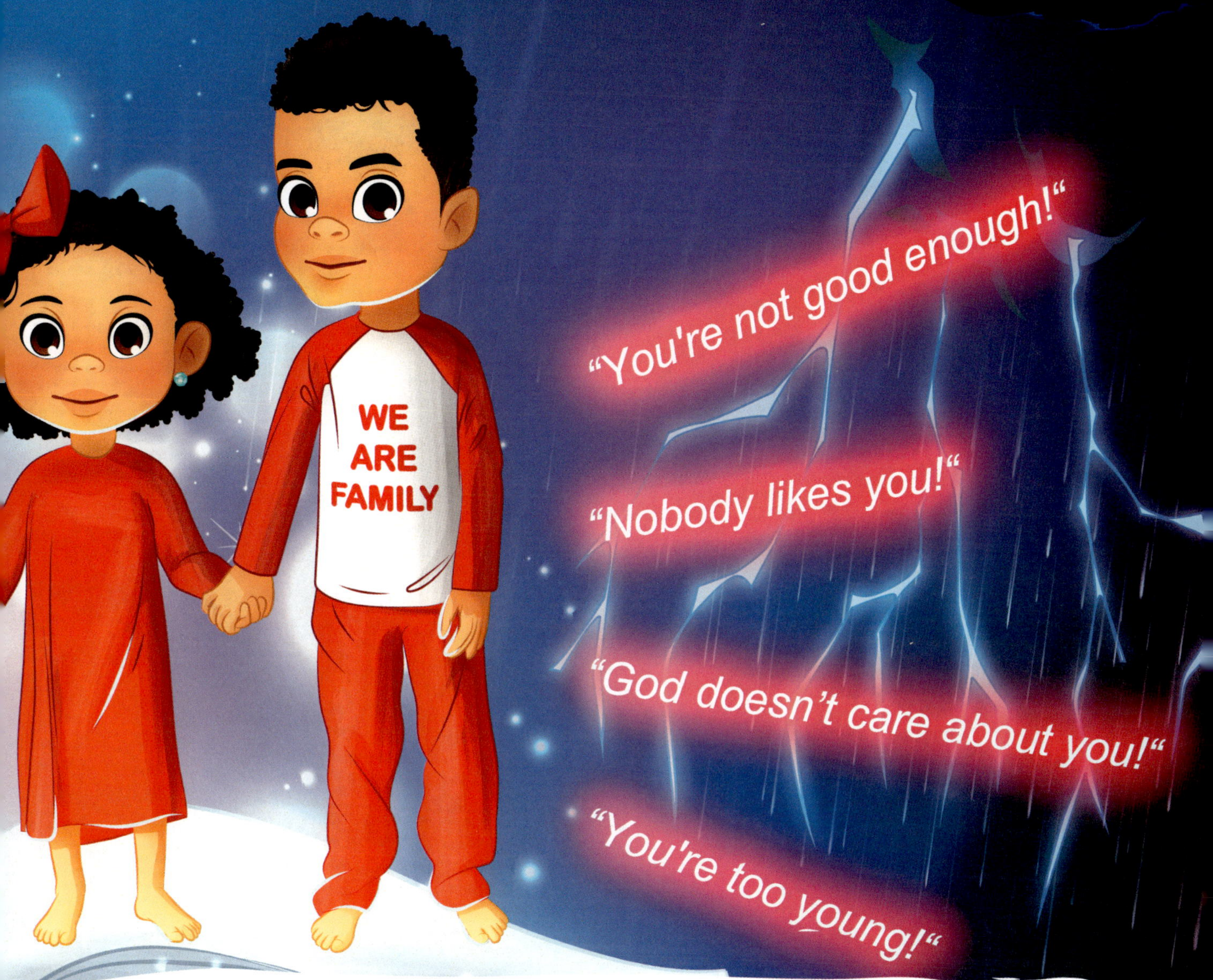

WE
ARE
FAMILY
“You're not good enough!“
“Nobody likes you!“
“God doesn’t care about you!“
“You're too young!“

“So, my dear brothers and sisters, because of all this, be strong and immovable. Do not allow anyone to change your mind. Always do your work well for the Lord. You know that whatever you do for Him will not be wasted.”

- 1 Corinthians 15:58 (NVL)

God will always love you, don't ever forget,
even if He hasn't answered your prayers yet.
Sometimes, He won't give you what you want at all,

You can pray whether you're happy, mad, or blue,
or when you need wisdom from the guy with a view.
Your prayers can be short, medium, or long,
it is your choice, and you cannot go wrong.
They can be perfectly silent or incredibly loud,
either way, it will make God proud.

Your eyes can be opened, or all the way closed,
you can be upset or completely composed.
Your hands can be folded or maybe not,
just try not to get lost in your own thought.
You can pray in a group or all on your own,
but when praying to God, you're never alone.

"Let us then approach God's throne of grace with confidence, so that we may receive mercy and find grace to help us in our time of need."
- Hebrews 4:16 (NIV)

"Don't worry about anything; instead, pray about everything. Tell God what you need, and thank him for all he has done."
- Philippians 4:6 (NLT)

Lord, please let me do well on my test.

God, I had a nightmare and I'm scared. Give me peace and fill me with happy thoughts.

You can pray in the evening, morning, or day, or whenever you need to keep bad thoughts away.

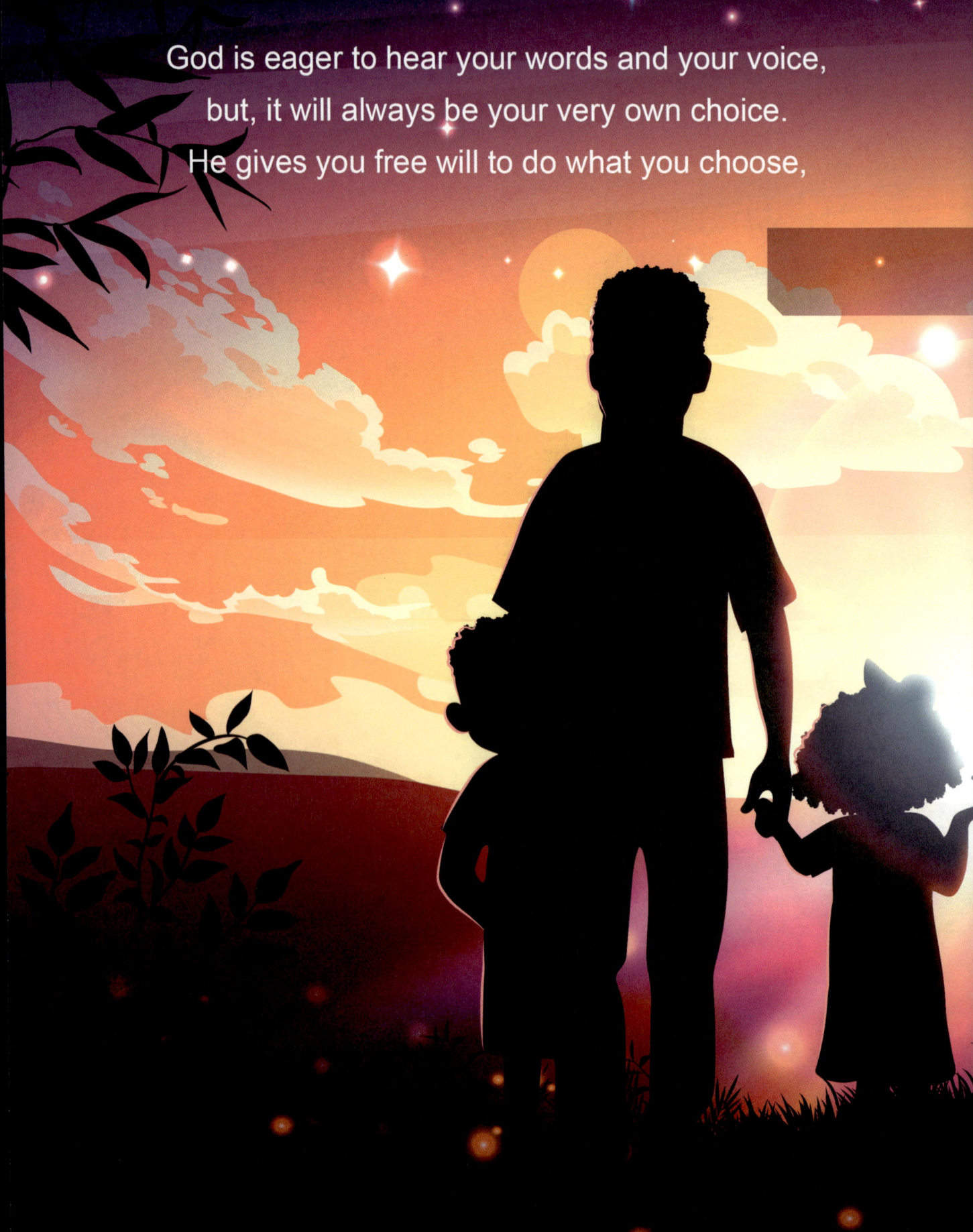

Praise, Confess, Thanks, Others, and You,
now you can teach people how to pray too.
You can follow these steps or create your own,
the goal is to spend time with God and not feel alone.
To help you remember how you can pray,
use this prayer hand to guide your way.

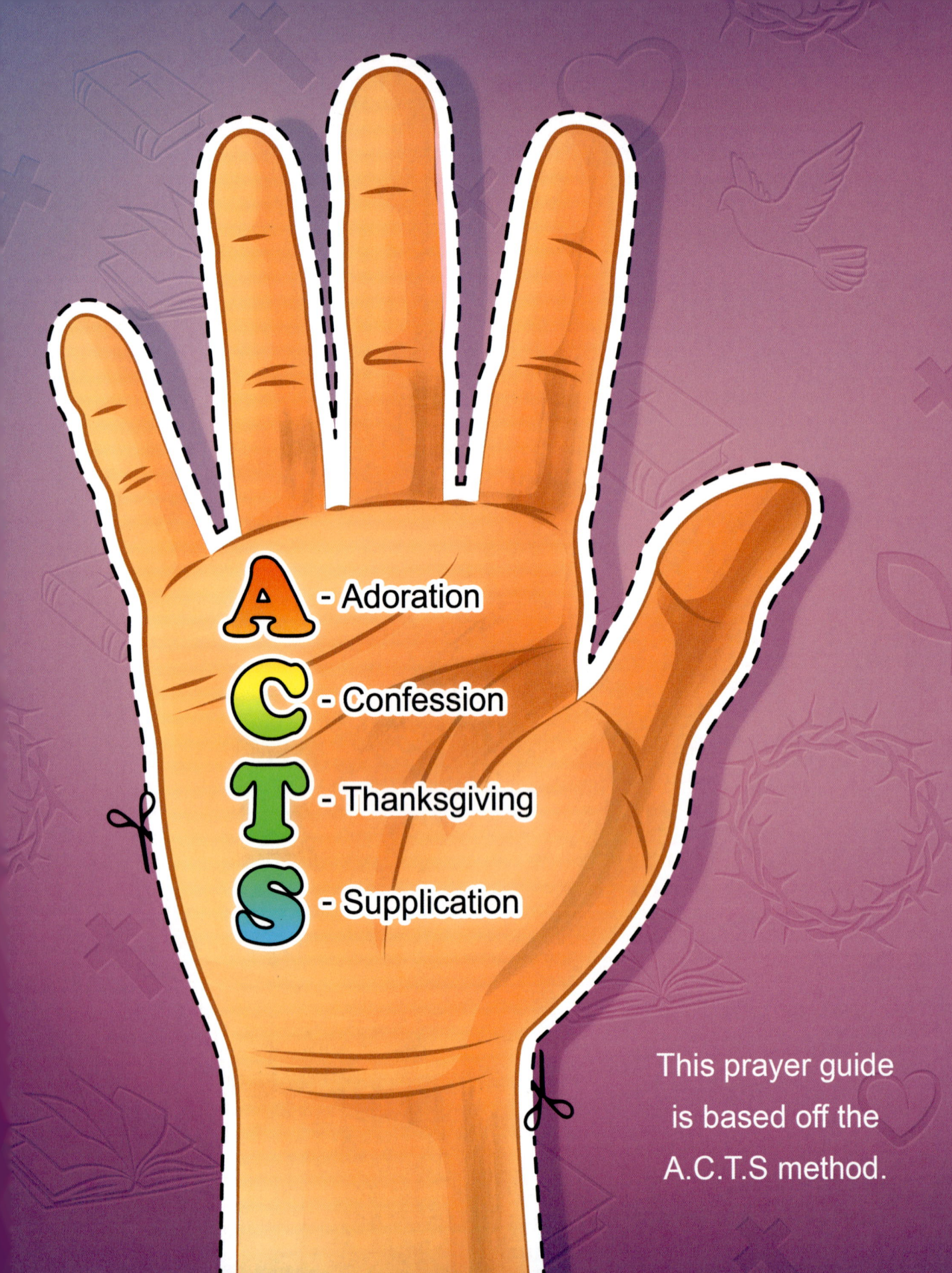

"So when you pray, you should pray like this: 'Our Father in heaven, we pray that your name will always be kept holy. We pray that your kingdom will come. We pray that what you want will be done, here on earth as it is in heaven. Give us the food we need for each day. Forgive the sins we have done, just as we have forgiven those who did wrong to us. And do not cause us to be tested; but save us from the Evil One.' [The kingdom, the power, and the glory are yours forever. Amen.]"

– Matthew 6:9-13 (ICB)

Made in the USA
Columbia, SC
20 November 2021